THE ANIMAL CHOIR OF BETHLEHEM

5 Bedtime Stories of the First Christmas

BLUME POTTER

INTRODUCTION

As you tuck your little ones into bed each night, there's a special kind of joy in sharing stories that not only entertain but also instill timeless values. The Animal Choir of Bethlehem: 5 Bedtime Stories of the First Christmas is more than just a collection of tales—it's a gentle journey through the wonder and meaning of the very first Christmas, told through the eyes of the animals who witnessed this miraculous event.

Each story in this book is crafted to captivate young hearts while teaching important lessons of humility, kindness, and the true spirit of giving. Your children and grandchildren will be drawn into the stable where Jesus was born, feeling the warmth of the cow's breath, hearing the joyful bleating of the sheep, and understanding the significance of even the smallest gifts, like the mouse's humble offering.

These stories are not only perfect for bedtime but also a wonderful way to introduce the younger generation to the profound message of the Bible in a way that is engaging and accessible. As they drift off to sleep, these tales will fill their dreams with the hope and promise that the birth of Jesus brought to the world.

We invite you to make The Animal Choir of Bethlehem a cherished part of your family's bedtime routine, creating memories that will last a lifetime and nurturing a love for the true meaning of Christmas in the hearts of those you love most.

CHAPTER 1:
THE DONKEY'S JOURNEY

In a small village, nestled among rolling hills, there lived a humble donkey. His days were simple, spent carrying loads of grain or pulling carts for the villagers. Yet, he was content, for he knew his work was important. Little did he know, a grander task awaited him—one that would change his life forever.

One crisp morning, the donkey was led by his master to a young woman named Mary. She had kind eyes and a gentle smile, and the donkey could sense something special about her. As she climbed onto his back, he felt a warmth in his heart, as if he was being called to do something more than his usual work.

The journey to Bethlehem was long and tiring, with rocky paths and steep hills. But the donkey trotted on, never slowing his pace. He could feel the precious burden he carried—a child not yet born but already full of wonder. The donkey didn't understand why, but he knew this journey was important. He was not just carrying Mary; he was part of something much bigger.

As they traveled, the donkey thought about his life. He had always been a simple creature, never seeking glory or praise. Yet now, he was carrying someone who would change the world. It made him realize that even the smallest and most humble creatures have a role to play in God's grand plan.

Finally, after days of walking, they reached Bethlehem. The town was crowded, and there was no room for Mary and her husband Joseph at the inn. But the donkey didn't worry. He knew that they would find a place, and that his part in this journey was almost complete.

They found shelter in a stable, surrounded by other animals. As Mary settled down to rest, the donkey stood nearby, watching over her. He felt a deep sense of peace, knowing he had done his duty. He may have been just a simple donkey, but on that night, he was part of something truly special.

And so, the donkey's journey came to an end. But in his heart, he knew that this was only the beginning of a much greater story—one that would be told for generations to come. The donkey had played his part, and he was content, knowing that even the smallest of roles can have a lasting impact in God's plan.

CHAPTER 2:
THE COW'S WARMTH

In the quiet stillness of the night, a gentle cow rested in the stable, her large eyes blinking softly in the dim light. She had spent the day grazing in the nearby fields, her life simple and routine. But tonight, something was different. The stable was unusually busy, with a young couple seeking shelter among the animals. The cow watched curiously as they settled down, sensing that something important was about to happen.

Soon, the young woman, Mary, gave birth to a baby—a tiny, fragile thing that seemed to radiate a soft glow. The cow felt a stir in her heart, a warmth that spread through her as she realized she was witnessing something extraordinary. She didn't know exactly who this child was, but she knew, deep down, that this was no ordinary night.

As the baby lay in the manger, the cow moved closer. She saw that the night air was cold, and the newborn shivered slightly. Instinctively, the cow leaned in, her warm breath puffing gently over the baby. The cow's breath created a cozy little cloud of warmth, surrounding the infant in a blanket of comfort.

The cow continued to breathe warmth over the baby, feeling a sense of purpose she had never known before. She was just a simple cow, used to giving milk and grazing in fields, but tonight, she had something precious to offer. Her warmth might seem like a small thing, but to the newborn child, it was everything.

As the baby settled into a peaceful sleep, the cow stood nearby, her heart filled with quiet joy. She had given what she could, and in doing so, she had become part of this wondrous moment. The cow understood that even the smallest gifts, when given with love, can make a world of difference.

And so, the cow stayed by the manger, her warmth and presence a silent offering of love. She may have been just a simple cow, but in that stable, on that night, she knew she was part of something far greater—a story of love and light that would shine for all time.

CHAPTER 3:
THE SHEEP'S SONG

On a hillside near Bethlehem, a flock of sheep rested under the twinkling stars. They were peaceful creatures, accustomed to the gentle rhythm of the night, with only the occasional rustle of leaves or the distant howl of a wolf to disturb their rest. But tonight, the stillness was suddenly broken by a light—brighter than any star they had ever seen.

The sheep lifted their heads as the sky above them filled with a chorus of angels. The angels sang a glorious song, announcing the birth of a Savior, and the shepherds who tended the sheep fell to their knees in awe. The sheep didn't fully understand what was happening, but they felt the joy in the air, a happiness that bubbled up inside them and made them want to join in.

Without thinking, the sheep began to bleat. At first, it was just one or two, but soon, the entire flock was bleating together, creating a melody that seemed to rise and blend with the angels' song. Their simple voices added a new layer of harmony, a humble but joyful praise that filled the night air.

The sheep's song was different from the angels'—not as grand or majestic—but it was full of sincerity and pure joy. The sheep were happy to be part of this moment, to share in the good news that had been brought to the world. Their song was a celebration, not just for the shepherds and the angels, but for all creatures great and small.

As the angels' song faded and the sky returned to its quiet darkness, the sheep continued their melody for a while longer, their voices carrying the echoes of the heavenly choir. They felt proud and content, knowing that they had played their part in this miraculous night.

The sheep understood that praising God didn't require grand gestures; even their simple song, offered with joy and sincerity, was enough. And so, with their hearts light and their spirits high, they returned to their peaceful grazing, knowing they had helped spread the good news in their own special way.

In that night of miracles, the sheep learned that everyone, no matter how small or humble, can offer praise to God and share in the joy of His love.

CHAPTER 4:
THE MOUSE'S GIFT

In the quiet corners of the stable, a little mouse scurried about, unnoticed by the larger animals. The mouse had lived in the stable for some time, making its home in a small hole in the wall. Life was simple for the mouse— finding bits of food and straw to build its nest—but tonight, the stable felt different. The air was filled with a sense of wonder, and the mouse could feel it too.

As the mouse peeked out from its hiding place, it saw the newborn baby lying in a manger, surrounded by the warm breath of the animals and the soft glow of the night. The mouse watched as the other animals offered their gifts of warmth and song, each contributing in their own way to welcome this special child.

The mouse wanted to give something too, but what could such a tiny creature offer? The mouse thought for a moment and then noticed a piece of golden straw, the perfect size for a small creature like itself. The mouse picked up the straw in its mouth and, with a heart full of love, scurried over to the manger.

Carefully, the mouse placed the piece of straw near the baby Jesus. It wasn't much, just a single strand, but it was the very best the mouse could offer. As the mouse looked up at the baby, it felt a warmth spread through its little body—a warmth that told the mouse its gift, though small, was accepted with love.

The mouse returned to its nest, feeling a sense of peace and happiness. It had given what it could, and that was enough. The mouse knew that in God's eyes, no gift is too small when given with a pure heart. The mouse's simple act of kindness was its way of showing love and devotion, just as important as any grander gesture.

As the night went on, the mouse snuggled into its nest, content and grateful. It understood that generosity isn't about the size of the gift, but the love with which it is given. And in that humble stable, the little mouse had given a gift that would be remembered in its own small way, as part of the greatest story ever told.

CHAPTER 5:
THE MORNING OF HOPE

As the first light of dawn began to creep over the hills of Bethlehem, the animals in the stable stirred from their rest. The night had been unlike any other, filled with wonder and awe. Each of them, from the humble donkey to the tiny mouse, had played a part in the miraculous events that had unfolded.

The stable was quiet now, the soft breathing of the baby Jesus the only sound in the early morning stillness. The donkey, cow, sheep, and mouse all looked toward the manger, where the newborn lay peacefully. They felt a deep sense of calm, as if the whole world had paused to take in this moment.

The donkey reflected on the journey it had made, feeling proud to have carried Mary safely to this place. The cow, still near the manger, continued to breathe warmth over the baby, content in its role of providing comfort. The sheep, their song of the night still echoing in their hearts, stood together in a gentle huddle. The mouse, nestled in its cozy nest, thought of the small straw it had given with so much love.

As the sunlight began to fill the stable, the animals sensed that this was more than just another morning. It was the beginning of something new, something filled with hope and promise. They didn't fully understand what the future would hold, but they knew that the world had changed in some profound way.

The animals were just simple creatures, but they understood the importance of what they had witnessed. The birth of this child brought a sense of peace and hope that filled the stable and beyond. They had been part of something extraordinary, something that would bring light to the whole world.

As the day began, the animals settled into the new morning with a deep sense of fulfillment. They knew that the baby in the manger was special, a promise of new beginnings and endless possibilities. The morning of hope had arrived, and with it, the dawn of a new era.

In their hearts, the animals carried the message of that night—a message of love, peace, and hope for all creation. And as they looked out into the brightening world, they knew that this hope would shine forever, just as the light of that first Christmas morning now filled the earth.

www.ingramcontent.com/pod-product-compliance
Lightning Source LLC
Chambersburg PA
CBHW080251180726
47999CB00019B/2827